50 Premium Fried Chicken Dinner Meal Ideas

By: Kelly Johnson

Table of Contents

- Classic Southern Fried Chicken
- Buttermilk-Brined Fried Chicken
- Nashville Hot Chicken
- Chicken and Waffles
- Fried Chicken with Honey Butter
- Spicy Cajun Fried Chicken
- Fried Chicken with Collard Greens
- Garlic Parmesan Fried Chicken
- Crispy Fried Chicken with Mashed Potatoes
- Southern Fried Chicken with Biscuits
- Lemon Herb Fried Chicken
- Fried Chicken Tenders with Sweet Potato Fries
- Fried Chicken with Cornbread Dressing
- Buttermilk Fried Chicken with Gravy
- Fried Chicken with Creamed Spinach
- Chicken Schnitzel with Potato Salad
- Chicken Fried Chicken with White Gravy
- Sweet and Sour Fried Chicken
- Fried Chicken with Charred Brussels Sprouts
- Spicy Fried Chicken with Pickles
- Buttermilk Fried Chicken with Mac and Cheese
- Fried Chicken with Bacon-Wrapped Asparagus
- Fried Chicken and Shrimp Po' Boy
- Fried Chicken with Jalapeño Cheddar Biscuits
- Fried Chicken with Roasted Garlic Mashed Potatoes
- Korean Fried Chicken with Kimchi Slaw
- Southern Fried Chicken with Green Beans Almondine
- Fried Chicken with Roasted Sweet Potatoes
- Buttermilk Fried Chicken with Grilled Corn
- Crispy Fried Chicken with Caesar Salad
- Fried Chicken with Avocado-Mango Salad
- Southern-Style Chicken and Dumplings
- Fried Chicken with Potato Wedges
- Fried Chicken and Gravy with Garlic Bread
- Lemon Pepper Fried Chicken with Cilantro Rice

- Fried Chicken with Corn on the Cob
- Hot Honey Fried Chicken with Grits
- Fried Chicken with Roasted Beet Salad
- Fried Chicken with Chili Garlic Noodles
- Fried Chicken with Cucumber and Tomato Salad
- Cajun Fried Chicken with Red Beans and Rice
- Fried Chicken with Spicy Ranch Dipping Sauce
- Fried Chicken with Cabbage Slaw
- Fried Chicken with Zucchini Fritters
- Crispy Fried Chicken with Creamy Corn
- Southern Fried Chicken with Bacon Gravy
- Spicy Fried Chicken with Pineapple Salsa
- Fried Chicken with Roasted Fingerling Potatoes
- Fried Chicken with Sweet Potato Hash
- Fried Chicken with Arugula and Pear Salad

Classic Southern Fried Chicken
Ingredients:

- 1 whole chicken, cut into pieces
- 2 cups buttermilk
- 1 tbsp hot sauce
- 2 cups all-purpose flour
- 1 tbsp paprika
- 1 tbsp garlic powder
- 1 tsp onion powder
- Salt and pepper to taste
- Vegetable oil for frying

Instructions:

1. In a bowl, combine the buttermilk, hot sauce, salt, and pepper. Submerge the chicken pieces in the mixture and refrigerate for at least 2 hours or overnight.
2. In a separate bowl, mix the flour, paprika, garlic powder, onion powder, salt, and pepper.
3. Heat vegetable oil in a large skillet or deep fryer to 350°F (175°C).
4. Dredge the marinated chicken in the flour mixture, pressing gently to coat. Fry in batches until golden brown and cooked through, about 10-12 minutes per side.
5. Drain on paper towels and serve hot.

Buttermilk-Brined Fried Chicken

Ingredients:

- 1 whole chicken, cut into pieces
- 3 cups buttermilk
- 2 tbsp salt
- 1 tbsp sugar
- 2 cups all-purpose flour
- 1 tbsp paprika
- 1 tsp cayenne pepper
- 1 tsp garlic powder
- Vegetable oil for frying

Instructions:

1. In a large bowl, whisk together buttermilk, salt, and sugar. Submerge the chicken in the brine and refrigerate for 4-6 hours.
2. In a shallow dish, combine the flour, paprika, cayenne, garlic powder, salt, and pepper.
3. Heat oil in a skillet to 350°F (175°C).
4. Remove the chicken from the brine, dredge it in the flour mixture, and fry until golden and crispy, about 10-12 minutes per side.
5. Drain on paper towels before serving.

Nashville Hot Chicken
Ingredients:

- 1 whole chicken, cut into pieces
- 2 cups buttermilk
- 1 tbsp paprika
- 1 tbsp garlic powder
- 1 tsp cayenne pepper
- 1 tbsp brown sugar
- 1 tsp salt
- 2 cups all-purpose flour
- Vegetable oil for frying
- 1/4 cup hot chicken oil (made with cayenne and spices)

Instructions:

1. Marinate the chicken in buttermilk, paprika, garlic powder, cayenne pepper, brown sugar, and salt for at least 4 hours or overnight.
2. In a shallow bowl, place the flour and season with salt and pepper.
3. Heat oil in a skillet to 350°F (175°C).
4. Dredge the chicken in the flour mixture, then fry until golden and crispy, about 10-12 minutes.
5. For the spicy oil, heat the hot chicken oil in a small pot and mix in cayenne and spices.
6. Brush the hot oil generously over the fried chicken before serving.

Chicken and Waffles
Ingredients:

- 4 pieces fried chicken
- 2 waffles (store-bought or homemade)
- Maple syrup
- 2 tbsp butter

Instructions:

1. Prepare the fried chicken and waffles.
2. Place a waffle on each plate, top with a piece of fried chicken.
3. Drizzle with maple syrup and a dollop of butter.
4. Serve immediately for a sweet and savory treat.

Fried Chicken with Honey Butter

Ingredients:

- 1 whole chicken, cut into pieces
- 2 cups buttermilk
- 1 tbsp hot sauce
- 2 cups all-purpose flour
- 1 tbsp garlic powder
- 1 tbsp paprika
- Salt and pepper to taste
- Vegetable oil for frying
- 1/2 cup unsalted butter, melted
- 2 tbsp honey

Instructions:

1. Marinate the chicken in buttermilk and hot sauce for at least 2 hours.
2. In a bowl, mix the flour, garlic powder, paprika, salt, and pepper.
3. Heat oil in a skillet to 350°F (175°C).
4. Dredge the chicken in the flour mixture, then fry until golden brown and cooked through, about 10-12 minutes per side.
5. In a small bowl, whisk together the melted butter and honey.
6. Drizzle the honey butter over the fried chicken and serve.

Spicy Cajun Fried Chicken
Ingredients:

- 1 whole chicken, cut into pieces
- 2 cups buttermilk
- 2 tbsp hot sauce
- 1 tbsp Cajun seasoning
- 2 cups all-purpose flour
- 1 tsp paprika
- 1 tsp garlic powder
- Salt and pepper to taste
- Vegetable oil for frying

Instructions:

1. Marinate the chicken in buttermilk, hot sauce, and Cajun seasoning for at least 2 hours.
2. In a bowl, mix the flour, paprika, garlic powder, salt, and pepper.
3. Heat oil in a skillet to 350°F (175°C).
4. Dredge the chicken in the flour mixture and fry until golden and crispy, about 10-12 minutes per side.
5. Drain on paper towels and serve hot.

Fried Chicken with Collard Greens
Ingredients:

- 1 whole chicken, cut into pieces
- 2 cups buttermilk
- 1 tbsp hot sauce
- 2 cups all-purpose flour
- 1 tbsp paprika
- 1 tbsp garlic powder
- Salt and pepper to taste
- Vegetable oil for frying
- 4 cups collard greens, chopped
- 1/2 onion, chopped
- 2 cloves garlic, minced
- 1 tbsp apple cider vinegar

Instructions:

1. Marinate the chicken in buttermilk and hot sauce for at least 2 hours.
2. In a bowl, mix the flour, paprika, garlic powder, salt, and pepper.
3. Heat oil in a skillet to 350°F (175°C).
4. Dredge the chicken in the flour mixture and fry until golden and crispy, about 10-12 minutes per side.
5. For the collard greens, sauté onion and garlic in a large pot until softened. Add the collard greens and cook until tender, about 15-20 minutes. Stir in the apple cider vinegar.
6. Serve the fried chicken with a side of collard greens.

Garlic Parmesan Fried Chicken

Ingredients:

- 1 whole chicken, cut into pieces
- 2 cups buttermilk
- 2 tbsp garlic powder
- 2 cups all-purpose flour
- 1 tbsp Italian seasoning
- Salt and pepper to taste
- Vegetable oil for frying
- 1/4 cup grated Parmesan cheese
- 2 tbsp melted butter

Instructions:

1. Marinate the chicken in buttermilk and garlic powder for at least 2 hours.
2. In a bowl, mix the flour, Italian seasoning, salt, and pepper.
3. Heat oil in a skillet to 350°F (175°C).
4. Dredge the chicken in the flour mixture and fry until golden and crispy, about 10-12 minutes per side.
5. In a small bowl, combine the melted butter and Parmesan cheese.
6. Drizzle the garlic Parmesan butter over the fried chicken and serve.

Crispy Fried Chicken with Mashed Potatoes

Ingredients:

- 1 whole chicken, cut into pieces
- 2 cups buttermilk
- 2 cups all-purpose flour
- 1 tbsp paprika
- 1 tbsp garlic powder
- Salt and pepper to taste
- Vegetable oil for frying
- 4 large potatoes, peeled and chopped
- 1/4 cup milk
- 2 tbsp butter
- Salt to taste

Instructions:

1. Marinate the chicken in buttermilk for at least 2 hours.
2. In a shallow bowl, mix the flour, paprika, garlic powder, salt, and pepper.
3. Heat oil in a skillet to 350°F (175°C).
4. Dredge the chicken in the flour mixture and fry until golden brown and crispy, about 10-12 minutes per side.
5. For the mashed potatoes, boil the chopped potatoes in salted water until tender, about 15 minutes. Drain and mash with milk, butter, and salt.
6. Serve the crispy fried chicken alongside the mashed potatoes.

Southern Fried Chicken with Biscuits
Ingredients:

- 1 whole chicken, cut into pieces
- 2 cups buttermilk
- 2 cups all-purpose flour
- 1 tbsp paprika
- 1 tbsp garlic powder
- Salt and pepper to taste
- Vegetable oil for frying
- 2 cups self-rising flour
- 1/4 cup cold butter, cubed
- 3/4 cup milk

Instructions:

1. Marinate the chicken in buttermilk for at least 2 hours.
2. In a shallow bowl, combine the flour, paprika, garlic powder, salt, and pepper.
3. Heat oil in a skillet to 350°F (175°C).
4. Dredge the chicken in the flour mixture and fry until golden and cooked through, about 10-12 minutes per side.
5. For the biscuits, combine self-rising flour and cold butter in a bowl. Cut in the butter until crumbly. Stir in the milk to form a dough.
6. Roll out the dough and cut into biscuits. Bake at 450°F (230°C) for 10-12 minutes.
7. Serve the fried chicken with hot biscuits.

Lemon Herb Fried Chicken

Ingredients:

- 1 whole chicken, cut into pieces
- 2 cups buttermilk
- 1 tbsp lemon zest
- 1 tbsp fresh thyme, chopped
- 2 cups all-purpose flour
- 1 tbsp garlic powder
- Salt and pepper to taste
- Vegetable oil for frying

Instructions:

1. Marinate the chicken in buttermilk, lemon zest, and thyme for at least 2 hours.
2. In a shallow bowl, combine the flour, garlic powder, salt, and pepper.
3. Heat oil in a skillet to 350°F (175°C).
4. Dredge the chicken in the flour mixture and fry until golden and crispy, about 10-12 minutes per side.
5. Serve the lemon herb fried chicken hot, garnished with extra thyme and lemon wedges.

Fried Chicken Tenders with Sweet Potato Fries
Ingredients:

- 2 lbs chicken tenders
- 2 cups buttermilk
- 2 cups all-purpose flour
- 1 tbsp paprika
- 1 tsp cayenne pepper
- Salt and pepper to taste
- Vegetable oil for frying
- 4 medium sweet potatoes, peeled and cut into fries
- 1 tbsp olive oil
- Salt to taste

Instructions:

1. Marinate the chicken tenders in buttermilk for at least 2 hours.
2. In a shallow bowl, combine the flour, paprika, cayenne, salt, and pepper.
3. Heat oil in a skillet to 350°F (175°C).
4. Dredge the chicken tenders in the flour mixture and fry until golden and crispy, about 4-6 minutes.
5. For the sweet potato fries, toss the cut sweet potatoes in olive oil and salt.
6. Bake at 425°F (220°C) for 20-25 minutes, flipping halfway through.
7. Serve the chicken tenders with hot sweet potato fries.

Fried Chicken with Cornbread Dressing
Ingredients:

- 1 whole chicken, cut into pieces
- 2 cups buttermilk
- 2 cups all-purpose flour
- 1 tbsp paprika
- 1 tbsp garlic powder
- Salt and pepper to taste
- Vegetable oil for frying
- 1 batch of cornbread, crumbled
- 1/2 onion, chopped
- 2 stalks celery, chopped
- 2 cups chicken broth
- 1 tsp sage
- 1 tsp thyme

Instructions:

1. Marinate the chicken in buttermilk for at least 2 hours.
2. In a shallow bowl, combine the flour, paprika, garlic powder, salt, and pepper.
3. Heat oil in a skillet to 350°F (175°C).
4. Dredge the chicken in the flour mixture and fry until golden and cooked through, about 10-12 minutes per side.
5. For the cornbread dressing, sauté the onion and celery in a skillet until softened.
6. Add crumbled cornbread, chicken broth, sage, and thyme. Stir and cook until the dressing is heated through.
7. Serve the fried chicken with cornbread dressing.

Buttermilk Fried Chicken with Gravy

Ingredients:

- 1 whole chicken, cut into pieces
- 2 cups buttermilk
- 2 cups all-purpose flour
- 1 tbsp paprika
- 1 tbsp garlic powder
- Salt and pepper to taste
- Vegetable oil for frying
- 2 tbsp butter
- 2 tbsp all-purpose flour
- 1 cup chicken broth
- Salt and pepper to taste

Instructions:

1. Marinate the chicken in buttermilk for at least 2 hours.
2. In a shallow bowl, combine the flour, paprika, garlic powder, salt, and pepper.
3. Heat oil in a skillet to 350°F (175°C).
4. Dredge the chicken in the flour mixture and fry until golden and crispy, about 10-12 minutes per side.
5. For the gravy, melt butter in a saucepan. Add flour and cook for 1-2 minutes.
6. Gradually add chicken broth while stirring to avoid lumps. Cook until thickened, about 5 minutes.
7. Serve the fried chicken with hot gravy.

Fried Chicken with Creamed Spinach
Ingredients:

- 1 whole chicken, cut into pieces
- 2 cups buttermilk
- 2 cups all-purpose flour
- 1 tbsp paprika
- 1 tbsp garlic powder
- Salt and pepper to taste
- Vegetable oil for frying
- 4 cups fresh spinach
- 1/2 cup heavy cream
- 2 tbsp butter
- Salt and pepper to taste

Instructions:

1. Marinate the chicken in buttermilk for at least 2 hours.
2. In a shallow bowl, combine the flour, paprika, garlic powder, salt, and pepper.
3. Heat oil in a skillet to 350°F (175°C).
4. Dredge the chicken in the flour mixture and fry until golden and crispy, about 10-12 minutes per side.
5. For the creamed spinach, melt butter in a skillet and sauté the spinach until wilted.
6. Add heavy cream, salt, and pepper, and cook until the mixture thickens, about 5 minutes.
7. Serve the fried chicken with a side of creamed spinach.

Chicken Schnitzel with Potato Salad

Ingredients:

- 4 boneless, skinless chicken breasts
- 2 cups breadcrumbs
- 2 eggs, beaten
- 1 cup all-purpose flour
- Salt and pepper to taste
- Vegetable oil for frying
- 4 large potatoes, peeled and boiled
- 1/2 cup mayonnaise
- 2 tbsp mustard
- 1/4 cup chopped pickles
- Salt and pepper to taste

Instructions:

1. Season the chicken breasts with salt and pepper.
2. Dredge the chicken in flour, dip in egg, and coat with breadcrumbs.
3. Heat oil in a skillet to 350°F (175°C). Fry the chicken schnitzels until golden and cooked through, about 4-5 minutes per side.
4. For the potato salad, mash the boiled potatoes with mayonnaise, mustard, chopped pickles, salt, and pepper.
5. Serve the chicken schnitzels with the potato salad on the side.

Chicken Fried Chicken with White Gravy
Ingredients:

- 4 boneless, skinless chicken breasts
- 2 cups buttermilk
- 2 cups all-purpose flour
- 1 tbsp garlic powder
- 1 tbsp onion powder
- 1 tsp paprika
- Salt and pepper to taste
- Vegetable oil for frying
- 2 tbsp butter
- 2 tbsp all-purpose flour
- 1 cup chicken broth
- 1/2 cup milk

Instructions:

1. Marinate the chicken breasts in buttermilk for at least 2 hours.
2. In a shallow bowl, combine flour, garlic powder, onion powder, paprika, salt, and pepper.
3. Heat oil in a skillet to 350°F (175°C). Dredge the chicken in the flour mixture and fry until golden and crispy, about 4-5 minutes per side.
4. For the gravy, melt butter in a saucepan, add flour, and cook for 1-2 minutes. Slowly whisk in chicken broth and milk. Cook until thickened.
5. Serve the chicken fried chicken with white gravy on top.

Sweet and Sour Fried Chicken
Ingredients:

- 1 whole chicken, cut into pieces
- 2 cups buttermilk
- 2 cups all-purpose flour
- 1 tbsp garlic powder
- 1 tbsp paprika
- Salt and pepper to taste
- Vegetable oil for frying
- 1/2 cup sugar
- 1/4 cup apple cider vinegar
- 1/4 cup ketchup
- 1 tbsp soy sauce
- 1 tbsp cornstarch

Instructions:

1. Marinate the chicken in buttermilk for at least 2 hours.
2. In a shallow bowl, combine flour, garlic powder, paprika, salt, and pepper.
3. Heat oil in a skillet to 350°F (175°C). Dredge the chicken in the flour mixture and fry until golden and crispy, about 10-12 minutes per side.
4. For the sauce, combine sugar, vinegar, ketchup, soy sauce, and cornstarch in a saucepan. Bring to a simmer and cook until thickened.
5. Toss the fried chicken in the sweet and sour sauce and serve.

Fried Chicken with Charred Brussels Sprouts

Ingredients:

- 1 whole chicken, cut into pieces
- 2 cups buttermilk
- 2 cups all-purpose flour
- 1 tbsp garlic powder
- 1 tbsp paprika
- Salt and pepper to taste
- Vegetable oil for frying
- 1 lb Brussels sprouts, trimmed and halved
- 1 tbsp olive oil
- Salt and pepper to taste

Instructions:

1. Marinate the chicken in buttermilk for at least 2 hours.
2. In a shallow bowl, combine flour, garlic powder, paprika, salt, and pepper.
3. Heat oil in a skillet to 350°F (175°C). Dredge the chicken in the flour mixture and fry until golden and crispy, about 10-12 minutes per side.
4. For the Brussels sprouts, heat olive oil in a skillet over high heat. Add the Brussels sprouts, cut side down, and cook until charred and tender, about 5-7 minutes.
5. Serve the fried chicken with charred Brussels sprouts on the side.

Spicy Fried Chicken with Pickles
Ingredients:

- 1 whole chicken, cut into pieces
- 2 cups buttermilk
- 2 cups all-purpose flour
- 1 tbsp paprika
- 1 tbsp cayenne pepper
- Salt and pepper to taste
- Vegetable oil for frying
- 1/2 cup pickles, sliced
- 1 tbsp hot sauce (optional)

Instructions:

1. Marinate the chicken in buttermilk for at least 2 hours.
2. In a shallow bowl, combine flour, paprika, cayenne, salt, and pepper.
3. Heat oil in a skillet to 350°F (175°C). Dredge the chicken in the flour mixture and fry until golden and crispy, about 10-12 minutes per side.
4. For the spicy chicken, drizzle with hot sauce (if desired) and serve with pickles on top or on the side.

Buttermilk Fried Chicken with Mac and Cheese
Ingredients:

- 1 whole chicken, cut into pieces
- 2 cups buttermilk
- 2 cups all-purpose flour
- 1 tbsp garlic powder
- 1 tbsp paprika
- Salt and pepper to taste
- Vegetable oil for frying
- 2 cups elbow macaroni
- 2 tbsp butter
- 2 cups milk
- 2 cups shredded cheddar cheese
- Salt and pepper to taste

Instructions:

1. Marinate the chicken in buttermilk for at least 2 hours.
2. In a shallow bowl, combine flour, garlic powder, paprika, salt, and pepper.
3. Heat oil in a skillet to 350°F (175°C). Dredge the chicken in the flour mixture and fry until golden and crispy, about 10-12 minutes per side.
4. For the mac and cheese, cook the macaroni according to package instructions. Drain and return to the pot.
5. Stir in butter, milk, and shredded cheddar cheese. Cook over low heat until creamy, then season with salt and pepper.
6. Serve the fried chicken with mac and cheese.

Fried Chicken with Bacon-Wrapped Asparagus
Ingredients:

- 1 whole chicken, cut into pieces
- 2 cups buttermilk
- 2 cups all-purpose flour
- 1 tbsp paprika
- 1 tbsp garlic powder
- Salt and pepper to taste
- Vegetable oil for frying
- 1 bunch asparagus, trimmed
- 8 slices bacon

Instructions:

1. Marinate the chicken in buttermilk for at least 2 hours.
2. In a shallow bowl, combine flour, paprika, garlic powder, salt, and pepper.
3. Heat oil in a skillet to 350°F (175°C). Dredge the chicken in the flour mixture and fry until golden and crispy, about 10-12 minutes per side.
4. For the bacon-wrapped asparagus, wrap each spear of asparagus with a slice of bacon.
5. Cook in a skillet over medium heat until the bacon is crispy, about 7-10 minutes.
6. Serve the fried chicken with bacon-wrapped asparagus on the side.

Fried Chicken and Shrimp Po' Boy
Ingredients:

- 2 chicken breasts, cut into strips
- 1/2 lb shrimp, peeled and deveined
- 2 cups buttermilk
- 2 cups all-purpose flour
- 1 tbsp paprika
- 1 tbsp garlic powder
- Salt and pepper to taste
- Vegetable oil for frying
- 4 hoagie rolls
- Lettuce, tomato, and pickles for garnish
- Remoulade sauce

Instructions:

1. Marinate the chicken strips and shrimp in buttermilk for at least 2 hours.
2. In a shallow bowl, combine flour, paprika, garlic powder, salt, and pepper.
3. Heat oil in a skillet to 350°F (175°C). Dredge the chicken and shrimp in the flour mixture and fry until golden and crispy, about 3-4 minutes per side for the chicken, and 2-3 minutes for the shrimp.
4. To assemble the Po' Boy, place fried chicken and shrimp in the hoagie rolls.
5. Garnish with lettuce, tomato, pickles, and a drizzle of remoulade sauce. Serve immediately.

Fried Chicken with Jalapeño Cheddar Biscuits
Ingredients:

- 1 whole chicken, cut into pieces
- 2 cups buttermilk
- 2 cups all-purpose flour
- 1 tbsp paprika
- 1 tbsp garlic powder
- Salt and pepper to taste
- Vegetable oil for frying
- 2 cups self-rising flour
- 1/2 cup grated cheddar cheese
- 2 jalapeños, diced
- 1/4 cup cold butter, cubed
- 3/4 cup milk

Instructions:

1. Marinate the chicken in buttermilk for at least 2 hours.
2. In a shallow bowl, combine flour, paprika, garlic powder, salt, and pepper.
3. Heat oil in a skillet to 350°F (175°C). Dredge the chicken in the flour mixture and fry until golden and crispy, about 10-12 minutes per side.
4. For the biscuits, combine self-rising flour, cheddar cheese, and diced jalapeños in a bowl. Cut in the cold butter until crumbly. Stir in the milk to form a dough.
5. Roll out the dough, cut into biscuits, and bake at 450°F (230°C) for 10-12 minutes.
6. Serve the fried chicken with jalapeño cheddar biscuits.

Fried Chicken with Roasted Garlic Mashed Potatoes
Ingredients:

- 1 whole chicken, cut into pieces
- 2 cups buttermilk
- 2 cups all-purpose flour
- 1 tbsp garlic powder
- 1 tbsp paprika
- Salt and pepper to taste
- Vegetable oil for frying
- 2 lbs potatoes, peeled and cubed
- 1 head garlic, roasted
- 1/2 cup butter
- 1/2 cup milk

Instructions:

1. Marinate the chicken in buttermilk for at least 2 hours.
2. In a shallow bowl, combine flour, garlic powder, paprika, salt, and pepper.
3. Heat oil in a skillet to 350°F (175°C). Dredge the chicken in the flour mixture and fry until golden and crispy, about 10-12 minutes per side.
4. For the mashed potatoes, roast the garlic by cutting off the top of the head, drizzling with olive oil, and roasting at 400°F (200°C) for 25-30 minutes.
5. Boil the potatoes until tender, then mash with butter, milk, and roasted garlic. Season with salt and pepper.
6. Serve the fried chicken with roasted garlic mashed potatoes.

Korean Fried Chicken with Kimchi Slaw

Ingredients:

- 1 whole chicken, cut into pieces
- 2 cups buttermilk
- 2 cups all-purpose flour
- 1 tbsp garlic powder
- 1 tbsp ginger powder
- 1 tbsp soy sauce
- 1 tbsp sesame oil
- Vegetable oil for frying
- 2 cups kimchi, chopped
- 1 cup shredded cabbage
- 1/4 cup mayonnaise
- 1 tbsp rice vinegar
- 1 tsp sugar
- 1 tbsp sesame seeds

Instructions:

1. Marinate the chicken in buttermilk for at least 2 hours.
2. In a shallow bowl, combine flour, garlic powder, ginger powder, soy sauce, and sesame oil.
3. Heat oil in a skillet to 350°F (175°C). Dredge the chicken in the flour mixture and fry until golden and crispy, about 10-12 minutes per side.
4. For the slaw, combine chopped kimchi, shredded cabbage, mayonnaise, rice vinegar, sugar, and sesame seeds.
5. Serve the fried chicken with the kimchi slaw.

Southern Fried Chicken with Green Beans Almondine

Ingredients:

- 1 whole chicken, cut into pieces
- 2 cups buttermilk
- 2 cups all-purpose flour
- 1 tbsp garlic powder
- 1 tbsp paprika
- Salt and pepper to taste
- Vegetable oil for frying
- 1 lb green beans, trimmed
- 1/4 cup sliced almonds
- 2 tbsp butter
- 1 tbsp lemon juice

Instructions:

1. Marinate the chicken in buttermilk for at least 2 hours.
2. In a shallow bowl, combine flour, garlic powder, paprika, salt, and pepper.
3. Heat oil in a skillet to 350°F (175°C). Dredge the chicken in the flour mixture and fry until golden and crispy, about 10-12 minutes per side.
4. For the green beans almondine, blanch the green beans in boiling water for 3-4 minutes, then sauté with butter and sliced almonds until golden.
5. Add lemon juice, and serve the fried chicken with green beans almondine.

Fried Chicken with Roasted Sweet Potatoes
Ingredients:

- 1 whole chicken, cut into pieces
- 2 cups buttermilk
- 2 cups all-purpose flour
- 1 tbsp garlic powder
- 1 tbsp paprika
- Salt and pepper to taste
- Vegetable oil for frying
- 2 lbs sweet potatoes, peeled and cubed
- 2 tbsp olive oil
- 1 tsp cinnamon
- 1 tbsp honey

Instructions:

1. Marinate the chicken in buttermilk for at least 2 hours.
2. In a shallow bowl, combine flour, garlic powder, paprika, salt, and pepper.
3. Heat oil in a skillet to 350°F (175°C). Dredge the chicken in the flour mixture and fry until golden and crispy, about 10-12 minutes per side.
4. For the roasted sweet potatoes, toss the cubes with olive oil, cinnamon, and a pinch of salt. Roast at 400°F (200°C) for 20-25 minutes, until tender.
5. Drizzle with honey, and serve the fried chicken with roasted sweet potatoes.

Buttermilk Fried Chicken with Grilled Corn

Ingredients:

- 1 whole chicken, cut into pieces
- 2 cups buttermilk
- 2 cups all-purpose flour
- 1 tbsp garlic powder
- 1 tbsp paprika
- Salt and pepper to taste
- Vegetable oil for frying
- 4 ears corn, husked
- 1 tbsp olive oil
- 1 tsp smoked paprika
- 1/4 cup butter

Instructions:

1. Marinate the chicken in buttermilk for at least 2 hours.
2. In a shallow bowl, combine flour, garlic powder, paprika, salt, and pepper.
3. Heat oil in a skillet to 350°F (175°C). Dredge the chicken in the flour mixture and fry until golden and crispy, about 10-12 minutes per side.
4. For the corn, brush the ears with olive oil and grill over medium heat for 8-10 minutes, turning occasionally.
5. Toss the grilled corn with smoked paprika and butter. Serve the fried chicken with grilled corn.

Crispy Fried Chicken with Caesar Salad

Ingredients:

- 1 whole chicken, cut into pieces
- 2 cups buttermilk
- 2 cups all-purpose flour
- 1 tbsp garlic powder
- 1 tbsp paprika
- Salt and pepper to taste
- Vegetable oil for frying
- 4 cups Romaine lettuce, chopped
- 1/2 cup Caesar dressing
- 1/4 cup grated Parmesan cheese
- Croutons

Instructions:

1. Marinate the chicken in buttermilk for at least 2 hours.
2. In a shallow bowl, combine flour, garlic powder, paprika, salt, and pepper.
3. Heat oil in a skillet to 350°F (175°C). Dredge the chicken in the flour mixture and fry until golden and crispy, about 10-12 minutes per side.
4. For the salad, toss the Romaine lettuce with Caesar dressing, grated Parmesan, and croutons.
5. Serve the fried chicken with Caesar salad.

Fried Chicken with Avocado-Mango Salad
Ingredients:

- 1 whole chicken, cut into pieces
- 2 cups buttermilk
- 2 cups all-purpose flour
- 1 tbsp garlic powder
- 1 tbsp paprika
- Salt and pepper to taste
- Vegetable oil for frying
- 1 avocado, diced
- 1 mango, diced
- 1/4 cup red onion, diced
- 2 tbsp lime juice
- Salt and pepper to taste

Instructions:

1. Marinate the chicken in buttermilk for at least 2 hours.
2. In a shallow bowl, combine flour, garlic powder, paprika, salt, and pepper.
3. Heat oil in a skillet to 350°F (175°C). Dredge the chicken in the flour mixture and fry until golden and crispy, about 10-12 minutes per side.
4. For the salad, combine diced avocado, mango, and red onion. Toss with lime juice, salt, and pepper.
5. Serve the fried chicken with avocado-mango salad.

Southern-Style Chicken and Dumplings
Ingredients:

- 1 whole chicken, cut into pieces
- 4 cups chicken broth
- 2 cups buttermilk
- 2 cups all-purpose flour
- 1 tbsp garlic powder
- 1 tbsp thyme
- Salt and pepper to taste
- 1/4 cup butter
- 1 cup milk
- 1 egg
- 1 cup frozen peas and carrots

Instructions:

1. In a large pot, bring the chicken broth to a boil. Add the chicken pieces and cook until tender, about 30 minutes.
2. Remove the chicken from the pot, shred the meat, and set aside.
3. In a bowl, combine flour, garlic powder, thyme, salt, and pepper. Add the buttermilk and mix into a dough.
4. Drop spoonfuls of the dough into the boiling broth and cook for 10-12 minutes, until the dumplings are fluffy.
5. Add the shredded chicken, peas, carrots, butter, and milk. Simmer until heated through. Serve hot.

Fried Chicken with Potato Wedges
Ingredients:

- 1 whole chicken, cut into pieces
- 2 cups buttermilk
- 2 cups all-purpose flour
- 1 tbsp garlic powder
- 1 tbsp paprika
- Salt and pepper to taste
- Vegetable oil for frying
- 4 large russet potatoes, cut into wedges
- 2 tbsp olive oil
- 1 tsp paprika
- 1 tsp garlic powder
- Salt and pepper to taste

Instructions:

1. Marinate the chicken in buttermilk for at least 2 hours.
2. In a shallow bowl, combine flour, garlic powder, paprika, salt, and pepper.
3. Heat oil in a skillet to 350°F (175°C). Dredge the chicken in the flour mixture and fry until golden and crispy, about 10-12 minutes per side.
4. For the potato wedges, toss the potato wedges with olive oil, paprika, garlic powder, salt, and pepper.
5. Roast in a 425°F (220°C) oven for 25-30 minutes, turning halfway through.
6. Serve the fried chicken with potato wedges.

Fried Chicken and Gravy with Garlic Bread
Ingredients:

- 1 whole chicken, cut into pieces
- 2 cups buttermilk
- 2 cups all-purpose flour
- 1 tbsp garlic powder
- 1 tbsp paprika
- Salt and pepper to taste
- Vegetable oil for frying
- 2 tbsp butter
- 2 tbsp all-purpose flour (for gravy)
- 2 cups chicken broth
- 2 garlic cloves, minced
- 4 slices of bread
- 2 tbsp butter (for garlic bread)

Instructions:

1. Marinate the chicken in buttermilk for at least 2 hours.
2. In a shallow bowl, combine flour, garlic powder, paprika, salt, and pepper.
3. Heat oil in a skillet to 350°F (175°C). Dredge the chicken in the flour mixture and fry until golden and crispy, about 10-12 minutes per side.
4. For the gravy, melt butter in a saucepan over medium heat. Whisk in the flour and cook for 1-2 minutes. Slowly whisk in the chicken broth and simmer until thickened.
5. For the garlic bread, spread butter on the bread slices and sprinkle with minced garlic. Toast in a 375°F (190°C) oven for 10-12 minutes.
6. Serve the fried chicken with gravy and garlic bread.

Lemon Pepper Fried Chicken with Cilantro Rice
Ingredients:

- 1 whole chicken, cut into pieces
- 2 cups buttermilk
- 2 cups all-purpose flour
- 1 tbsp garlic powder
- 1 tbsp lemon pepper seasoning
- Salt to taste
- Vegetable oil for frying
- 2 cups rice
- 1 tbsp butter
- 1/4 cup chopped cilantro
- Zest of 1 lemon
- Juice of 1 lemon

Instructions:

1. Marinate the chicken in buttermilk for at least 2 hours.
2. In a shallow bowl, combine flour, garlic powder, lemon pepper seasoning, and salt.
3. Heat oil in a skillet to 350°F (175°C). Dredge the chicken in the flour mixture and fry until golden and crispy, about 10-12 minutes per side.
4. For the rice, cook the rice according to package directions. Once cooked, stir in butter, chopped cilantro, lemon zest, and lemon juice.
5. Serve the fried chicken with cilantro rice.

Fried Chicken with Corn on the Cob
Ingredients:

- 1 whole chicken, cut into pieces
- 2 cups buttermilk
- 2 cups all-purpose flour
- 1 tbsp garlic powder
- 1 tbsp paprika
- Salt and pepper to taste
- Vegetable oil for frying
- 4 ears corn, husked
- 2 tbsp butter
- 1 tsp paprika
- Salt and pepper to taste

Instructions:

1. Marinate the chicken in buttermilk for at least 2 hours.
2. In a shallow bowl, combine flour, garlic powder, paprika, salt, and pepper.
3. Heat oil in a skillet to 350°F (175°C). Dredge the chicken in the flour mixture and fry until golden and crispy, about 10-12 minutes per side.
4. Boil or grill the corn on the cob until tender, about 8-10 minutes.
5. Brush the corn with butter and sprinkle with paprika, salt, and pepper.
6. Serve the fried chicken with corn on the cob.

Hot Honey Fried Chicken with Grits
Ingredients:

- 1 whole chicken, cut into pieces
- 2 cups buttermilk
- 2 cups all-purpose flour
- 1 tbsp garlic powder
- 1 tbsp paprika
- Salt and pepper to taste
- Vegetable oil for frying
- 1/2 cup honey
- 1/4 tsp cayenne pepper
- 2 cups stone-ground grits
- 4 cups water
- 1/2 cup cream
- 2 tbsp butter

Instructions:

1. Marinate the chicken in buttermilk for at least 2 hours.
2. In a shallow bowl, combine flour, garlic powder, paprika, salt, and pepper.
3. Heat oil in a skillet to 350°F (175°C). Dredge the chicken in the flour mixture and fry until golden and crispy, about 10-12 minutes per side.
4. For the hot honey, combine honey and cayenne pepper in a saucepan and heat over low heat until warm.
5. For the grits, bring water to a boil and stir in grits. Reduce to a simmer and cook, stirring occasionally, for 25-30 minutes. Stir in cream and butter once cooked.
6. Serve the fried chicken with grits and drizzle with hot honey.

Fried Chicken with Roasted Beet Salad

Ingredients:

- 1 whole chicken, cut into pieces
- 2 cups buttermilk
- 2 cups all-purpose flour
- 1 tbsp garlic powder
- 1 tbsp paprika
- Salt and pepper to taste
- Vegetable oil for frying
- 2 medium beets, roasted and sliced
- 4 cups mixed greens
- 1/4 cup goat cheese, crumbled
- 1/4 cup balsamic vinaigrette

Instructions:

1. Marinate the chicken in buttermilk for at least 2 hours.
2. In a shallow bowl, combine flour, garlic powder, paprika, salt, and pepper.
3. Heat oil in a skillet to 350°F (175°C). Dredge the chicken in the flour mixture and fry until golden and crispy, about 10-12 minutes per side.
4. For the salad, roast the beets by wrapping them in foil and baking at 400°F (200°C) for 45-60 minutes. Slice and toss with mixed greens, goat cheese, and balsamic vinaigrette.
5. Serve the fried chicken with roasted beet salad.

Fried Chicken with Chili Garlic Noodles

Ingredients:

- 1 whole chicken, cut into pieces
- 2 cups buttermilk
- 2 cups all-purpose flour
- 1 tbsp garlic powder
- 1 tbsp paprika
- Salt and pepper to taste
- Vegetable oil for frying
- 8 oz egg noodles
- 2 tbsp olive oil
- 2 garlic cloves, minced
- 1 tbsp chili paste
- 2 tbsp soy sauce
- 1 tbsp sesame oil
- 1/4 cup green onions, sliced

Instructions:

1. Marinate the chicken in buttermilk for at least 2 hours.
2. In a shallow bowl, combine flour, garlic powder, paprika, salt, and pepper.
3. Heat oil in a skillet to 350°F (175°C). Dredge the chicken in the flour mixture and fry until golden and crispy, about 10-12 minutes per side.
4. For the noodles, cook the egg noodles according to package directions. Drain and set aside.
5. In a pan, heat olive oil over medium heat. Add garlic and sauté for 1 minute. Stir in chili paste, soy sauce, and sesame oil. Add the cooked noodles and toss to coat.
6. Serve the fried chicken with chili garlic noodles.

Fried Chicken with Cucumber and Tomato Salad

Ingredients:

- 1 whole chicken, cut into pieces
- 2 cups buttermilk
- 2 cups all-purpose flour
- 1 tbsp garlic powder
- 1 tbsp paprika
- Salt and pepper to taste
- Vegetable oil for frying
- 2 cups cherry tomatoes, halved
- 1 cucumber, sliced
- 1/4 cup red onion, thinly sliced
- 2 tbsp olive oil
- 1 tbsp red wine vinegar
- Salt and pepper to taste

Instructions:

1. Marinate the chicken in buttermilk for at least 2 hours.
2. In a shallow bowl, combine flour, garlic powder, paprika, salt, and pepper.
3. Heat oil in a skillet to 350°F (175°C). Dredge the chicken in the flour mixture and fry until golden and crispy, about 10-12 minutes per side.
4. For the salad, combine the tomatoes, cucumber, and red onion. Drizzle with olive oil and red wine vinegar, then season with salt and pepper.
5. Serve the fried chicken with cucumber and tomato salad.

Cajun Fried Chicken with Red Beans and Rice

Ingredients:

- 1 whole chicken, cut into pieces
- 2 cups buttermilk
- 2 cups all-purpose flour
- 1 tbsp Cajun seasoning
- 1 tsp garlic powder
- Salt and pepper to taste
- Vegetable oil for frying
- 2 cups cooked rice
- 1 can red beans, drained and rinsed
- 1/4 cup green bell pepper, chopped
- 1/4 cup celery, chopped
- 1/4 cup onion, chopped
- 1 clove garlic, minced
- 1 tsp thyme
- 1/2 tsp paprika
- 1/2 tsp cayenne pepper
- 1 tbsp vegetable oil

Instructions:

1. Marinate the chicken in buttermilk for at least 2 hours.
2. In a shallow bowl, combine flour, Cajun seasoning, garlic powder, salt, and pepper.
3. Heat oil in a skillet to 350°F (175°C). Dredge the chicken in the flour mixture and fry until golden and crispy, about 10-12 minutes per side.
4. For the red beans and rice, heat oil in a pan over medium heat. Add the bell pepper, celery, onion, and garlic. Sauté until softened, about 5 minutes. Add the red beans, thyme, paprika, cayenne, and cooked rice. Stir to combine and cook for another 5 minutes.
5. Serve the fried chicken alongside the red beans and rice.

Fried Chicken with Spicy Ranch Dipping Sauce
Ingredients:

- 1 whole chicken, cut into pieces
- 2 cups buttermilk
- 2 cups all-purpose flour
- 1 tbsp garlic powder
- 1 tbsp paprika
- Salt and pepper to taste
- Vegetable oil for frying
- 1/2 cup ranch dressing
- 1 tbsp hot sauce
- 1/4 tsp cayenne pepper

Instructions:

1. Marinate the chicken in buttermilk for at least 2 hours.
2. In a shallow bowl, combine flour, garlic powder, paprika, salt, and pepper.
3. Heat oil in a skillet to 350°F (175°C). Dredge the chicken in the flour mixture and fry until golden and crispy, about 10-12 minutes per side.
4. For the dipping sauce, combine ranch dressing, hot sauce, and cayenne pepper in a small bowl.
5. Serve the fried chicken with the spicy ranch dipping sauce.

Fried Chicken with Cabbage Slaw
Ingredients:

- 1 whole chicken, cut into pieces
- 2 cups buttermilk
- 2 cups all-purpose flour
- 1 tbsp garlic powder
- 1 tbsp paprika
- Salt and pepper to taste
- Vegetable oil for frying
- 2 cups shredded cabbage
- 1/4 cup shredded carrots
- 1/4 cup mayonnaise
- 1 tbsp apple cider vinegar
- 1 tsp sugar
- Salt and pepper to taste

Instructions:

1. Marinate the chicken in buttermilk for at least 2 hours.
2. In a shallow bowl, combine flour, garlic powder, paprika, salt, and pepper.
3. Heat oil in a skillet to 350°F (175°C). Dredge the chicken in the flour mixture and fry until golden and crispy, about 10-12 minutes per side.
4. For the cabbage slaw, mix together the cabbage, carrots, mayonnaise, apple cider vinegar, sugar, salt, and pepper in a bowl.
5. Serve the fried chicken with the cabbage slaw.

Fried Chicken with Zucchini Fritters

Ingredients:

- 1 whole chicken, cut into pieces
- 2 cups buttermilk
- 2 cups all-purpose flour
- 1 tbsp garlic powder
- 1 tbsp paprika
- Salt and pepper to taste
- Vegetable oil for frying
- 2 medium zucchinis, grated
- 1/4 cup grated parmesan cheese
- 1/2 cup flour
- 1 egg
- Salt and pepper to taste

Instructions:

1. Marinate the chicken in buttermilk for at least 2 hours.
2. In a shallow bowl, combine flour, garlic powder, paprika, salt, and pepper.
3. Heat oil in a skillet to 350°F (175°C). Dredge the chicken in the flour mixture and fry until golden and crispy, about 10-12 minutes per side.
4. For the zucchini fritters, squeeze out excess moisture from the grated zucchini. In a bowl, combine zucchini, parmesan cheese, flour, egg, salt, and pepper. Form the mixture into small patties.
5. Fry the zucchini fritters in hot oil until crispy and golden, about 2-3 minutes per side.
6. Serve the fried chicken with zucchini fritters.

Crispy Fried Chicken with Creamy Corn

Ingredients:

- 1 whole chicken, cut into pieces
- 2 cups buttermilk
- 2 cups all-purpose flour
- 1 tbsp garlic powder
- 1 tbsp paprika
- Salt and pepper to taste
- Vegetable oil for frying
- 2 cups frozen corn kernels
- 1/2 cup heavy cream
- 1 tbsp butter
- 1/2 tsp garlic powder
- Salt and pepper to taste

Instructions:

1. Marinate the chicken in buttermilk for at least 2 hours.
2. In a shallow bowl, combine flour, garlic powder, paprika, salt, and pepper.
3. Heat oil in a skillet to 350°F (175°C). Dredge the chicken in the flour mixture and fry until golden and crispy, about 10-12 minutes per side.
4. For the creamy corn, melt butter in a saucepan over medium heat. Add the corn and garlic powder and sauté for 2 minutes. Add heavy cream, salt, and pepper. Simmer for 5 minutes, stirring occasionally.
5. Serve the fried chicken with creamy corn.

Southern Fried Chicken with Bacon Gravy

Ingredients:

- 1 whole chicken, cut into pieces
- 2 cups buttermilk
- 2 cups all-purpose flour
- 1 tbsp garlic powder
- 1 tbsp paprika
- Salt and pepper to taste
- Vegetable oil for frying
- 4 slices bacon, chopped
- 2 tbsp all-purpose flour
- 1 cup milk
- Salt and pepper to taste

Instructions:

1. Marinate the chicken in buttermilk for at least 2 hours.
2. In a shallow bowl, combine flour, garlic powder, paprika, salt, and pepper.
3. Heat oil in a skillet to 350°F (175°C). Dredge the chicken in the flour mixture and fry until golden and crispy, about 10-12 minutes per side.
4. For the bacon gravy, cook the chopped bacon in a skillet over medium heat until crispy. Remove the bacon and set aside, leaving the bacon drippings in the pan.
5. Add 2 tablespoons of flour to the drippings and whisk to make a roux. Slowly add the milk, whisking constantly, until the gravy thickens. Season with salt and pepper.
6. Serve the fried chicken with the bacon gravy and garnish with crispy bacon.

Spicy Fried Chicken with Pineapple Salsa
Ingredients:

- 1 whole chicken, cut into pieces
- 2 cups buttermilk
- 2 cups all-purpose flour
- 1 tbsp cayenne pepper
- 1 tbsp garlic powder
- Salt and pepper to taste
- Vegetable oil for frying
- 1 cup pineapple, diced
- 1/4 cup red onion, finely chopped
- 1/4 cup cilantro, chopped
- 1 jalapeño, deseeded and minced
- 1 tbsp lime juice
- Salt to taste

Instructions:

1. Marinate the chicken in buttermilk for at least 2 hours.
2. In a shallow bowl, combine flour, cayenne pepper, garlic powder, salt, and pepper.
3. Heat oil in a skillet to 350°F (175°C). Dredge the chicken in the flour mixture and fry until golden and crispy, about 10-12 minutes per side.
4. For the pineapple salsa, combine diced pineapple, red onion, cilantro, jalapeño, lime juice, and salt in a bowl. Stir to combine.
5. Serve the spicy fried chicken with the pineapple salsa on top.

Fried Chicken with Roasted Fingerling Potatoes
Ingredients:

- 1 whole chicken, cut into pieces
- 2 cups buttermilk
- 2 cups all-purpose flour
- 1 tbsp garlic powder
- 1 tbsp paprika
- Salt and pepper to taste
- Vegetable oil for frying
- 1 lb fingerling potatoes, halved
- 2 tbsp olive oil
- 1 tsp rosemary
- Salt and pepper to taste

Instructions:

1. Marinate the chicken in buttermilk for at least 2 hours.
2. In a shallow bowl, combine flour, garlic powder, paprika, salt, and pepper.
3. Heat oil in a skillet to 350°F (175°C). Dredge the chicken in the flour mixture and fry until golden and crispy, about 10-12 minutes per side.
4. For the roasted fingerling potatoes, preheat the oven to 400°F (200°C). Toss the fingerling potatoes with olive oil, rosemary, salt, and pepper. Roast for 25-30 minutes, or until tender and crispy.
5. Serve the fried chicken with the roasted fingerling potatoes.

Fried Chicken with Sweet Potato Hash
Ingredients:

- 1 whole chicken, cut into pieces
- 2 cups buttermilk
- 2 cups all-purpose flour
- 1 tbsp garlic powder
- 1 tbsp paprika
- Salt and pepper to taste
- Vegetable oil for frying
- 2 medium sweet potatoes, peeled and diced
- 1 red bell pepper, diced
- 1 onion, diced
- 2 tbsp olive oil
- Salt and pepper to taste

Instructions:

1. Marinate the chicken in buttermilk for at least 2 hours.
2. In a shallow bowl, combine flour, garlic powder, paprika, salt, and pepper.
3. Heat oil in a skillet to 350°F (175°C). Dredge the chicken in the flour mixture and fry until golden and crispy, about 10-12 minutes per side.
4. For the sweet potato hash, heat olive oil in a large skillet over medium heat. Add the diced sweet potatoes and cook for 10-12 minutes, or until tender. Add the bell pepper and onion and cook for an additional 5 minutes. Season with salt and pepper.
5. Serve the fried chicken with the sweet potato hash.

Fried Chicken with Arugula and Pear Salad
Ingredients:

- 1 whole chicken, cut into pieces
- 2 cups buttermilk
- 2 cups all-purpose flour
- 1 tbsp garlic powder
- 1 tbsp paprika
- Salt and pepper to taste
- Vegetable oil for frying
- 4 cups arugula
- 2 pears, sliced
- 1/4 cup candied pecans
- 1/4 cup blue cheese crumbles
- 2 tbsp balsamic vinaigrette

Instructions:

1. Marinate the chicken in buttermilk for at least 2 hours.
2. In a shallow bowl, combine flour, garlic powder, paprika, salt, and pepper.
3. Heat oil in a skillet to 350°F (175°C). Dredge the chicken in the flour mixture and fry until golden and crispy, about 10-12 minutes per side.
4. For the salad, toss the arugula, sliced pears, candied pecans, and blue cheese in a bowl. Drizzle with balsamic vinaigrette and toss to combine.
5. Serve the fried chicken with the arugula and pear salad.

These flavorful pairings offer a variety of savory, sweet, and crunchy sides to complement crispy fried chicken.